M000190389

Landing In New Jersey
With Soft Hands

9/12/97

For Josh ~

Fellow swimmer
in this river .
good luck writing .

BJ

Landing In New Jersey
With Soft Hands

BJ Ward

North Atlantic Books
Berkeley, CA

Landing In New Jersey With Soft Hands

Copyright © 1994 BJ Ward. All rights reserved. No part of this publication may be repro-duced or transmitted in any form or by any means, electronic or mechanical, including photocopy, or any information storage or retrieval system, without written permission of the publisher. Printed in the United States of America.

Published by
North Atlantic Books
P.O. Box 12327
Berkeley, California 94701–9998

Cover and book design by Catherine Campaigne

Landing In New Jersey With Soft Hands is sponsored by The Society for the Study of Native Arts and Sciences, a nonprofit educational corporation whose goals are to develop an edu-cational and crosscultural perspective linking various scientific, social and artistic fields; to nurture a holistic view of arts, sciences, humanities, and healing; and to publish and distribute literature on the relationship of mind, body and nature.

ISBN: 1-55643-184-8

1   2   3   4   5   6   7   8   9   /   98   97   96   95   94

Contents

For My Mother

Gratitudes

Thanks to all my teachers, great and small, and especially to Ben Lapinski, who taught me how to learn. Thanks to Ed Romond, who gave me wings, to Stephen Dunn, who taught me to fly, and Stephen Dobyns, who taught me to land.

Much gratitude to N.F. Ingram, Charles Rafferty, George Cruys, Heather Davis, Craig Brown, Jamie Lane, Annabelle Honza, Ron Henry, and Eileen Moeller, all of whom have given generous advice on some of these poems.

Thanks to Tim, Kevin, and Eric, who helped me sin as well as I did, and Paulie, who never shook his head at me. Not once.

Thanks to Glen Burtnik and John Eddie for all the music.

Thanks to all the brothers and sisters at the IKA and the owls. Who? The owls. Who?

Introduction

Idaho trails from my left pennyloafer,
Arizona from my right.
A Nevada waitress hangs from my heart.
The many loves of the many states
are crushed into my wash-needing socks.
My ears still cling to the musicians
I've loved in these many places.
There is here, in my pocket,
a momento for you.
It is a sound,
and if you could open it,
your very palms would shiver
with what my travels play
in the small, well-boned ears
you have in your hips,
     your legs, your ankles, your feet.

Are you dancing?

Hometown: Alliance, New Jersey

On the fading streets of my Alliance
the girls with soccer balls cross puddles
in their own little rivers of desperation—
each one a teenager, each one inheriting
the teen-age world. The mechanics who watch
with eyes as big as their mouths close the hoods
on cars as they have closed the hoods
on their women, working on them as needed.
Everything is beating, beating, beating
in this town. The sun has become relentless
in its insistence to pin us. The wildflower garden
is overtaking the grammar school.
And the bed above the tavern cracked
the floorboards when another man clenched up
into a huge sexual fist with MiMi—
Alliance's first hooker. She's so good
even the German cop likes her. Right now
a man hands her ten dollars and she
kneels in front of him, changing yet another thing.
But what has changed here? The brant geese
still return in May, the borders of the river banks
still break down every rainfall. Dinner is being cooked,
the cooper is closing shop, and in the barnyard
a chicken discovers a worm it finds delicious.

The First Thing To Say

At Port Colden Grammar School
we were filed down
the steps into cement halls
when the blasting of bells
crashed through on playtime—
how one drawn out bell meant Fire
and Fire meant fresh air
while three quick punches meant Air Raid.
This is how we learned the rhythm of bells,
crouching in half-light with our books
over our heads, hoping that hard knowledge
could stop bricks and cinders.
And with the bells intruding on us
like the aircraft closing in above,
everyone was laughing at Jimmy Muzecki
who could make people laugh at anything,
even things that weren't funny.
As I crouched I tried to think
of the first thing to say
in this commotion, how this could be it—
no more milk shakes or turtle-hunting,
no more dodgeball, no pez,
no Christmas—the big IT
and we're just down here giggling.
Now Carey Kresgie was punching Farting Charley
and Charley was farting.
Everyone was happy with this.
The first thing to say, I thought,
would have to do with the stupid,
the clanging overhead—cacophony

in a space where air should not be raided,
where safety had to do with depth and books.
I would tell them, I would tell them
all. But Jake and Nate were standing
and sitting, sometimes flailing
their arms—daring to be picked off
by Miss Skunkmuffin—and everyone was dying
with laughter.
                So the first thing to say
would have to be silly, I thought,
something for whoever would listen,
tired of bells, wanting to hear something
that had nothing to do with the crumbs of cement
that would drop about us.
                                Above me,
I could hear the engines approaching, unstoppable
as the locusts; I imagined the bomb doors
opening, spilling their shiny, jewel-like cargo
onto the courts and markets and schools below,
onto Mr. Johnson sweeping his splintered stoop,
onto Mrs. Wimfleson and her hairless poodle "Smooches",
onto my mother, onto Carey Kresgie's mother,
onto all our mothers and fathers and sons and daughters—
unloading their godawful yawns and guffaws
to shake the words right out of my mouth.

On The Last Day of the End of the World

The rock is what he knew—
he knew the hard weight of rock.
This went on for years—
the slow, uneasy rolling of weightedness
        followed by an unwinding, what else?
And for years he studied it—
how everything pushed will eventually push back—
and he knew nothing of breaking,
        of suddenly not pushing
                or not being pushed,
and so he decided nothing.
To him there was hill.
And there was rock.
He used to think that rock was his burden,
but now he knew it was hill.
He was tired of pushing,
        yes, and of being pushed,
and he knew the rock wasn't tired
        of being rock,
nor the hill tired of sloping.
By now he had forgotten
why he pushed the rock
so when someone yelled to him,
"Why do you push? It will only push back
        and the world is ending,"
he, who knew nothing of ending,
        looked up and said,
                "Leave me alone."

And so the people left the myth—
buildings fell, the ground split,
and the planet rolled across the surface
of the sun, becoming part of that new fire,
losing its old sensibilities, and, against
the efforts of all that had been there, ended.

Shakespeare as a Waiter

He was tired of the old ladies
   wanting cappuccino, of the little kids
with their chocolate milk or two cherries
   on a plastic dagger—anything to consume
his time while he had more important things
   to do—a fair lady in booth three was dying
for a reuben, and twelve lit professors
   wanted another round of ale and song in the lounge,
and his entire tip probably depended on it.
   This is where he started to learn timing—
when to allow the waiting, when to deliver
   what will last a while.
His boss started yelling—"Shakespeare!
   Bus your tables!" He was tired of this too.
He was tired of picking up and wiping down,
   tired of people's half-eaten burgers,
tired of salad dressing, tired of the spit,
   tired of the cooks who called him "Willy,"
tired of directing people to the bathroom
   when he had so much more
direction to offer. But he didn't reject this—
   none of it. Instead, he took it in,
studied it until he understood it.

In his mind, things grew large—
   first nothing, then nothing
became an ocean
   dotted with islands—
each island had a name—

Venice, love, Denmark—

    a dark count started to form,
  witches sang,
        stars crossed,

and Shakespeare,
      between the napkins and ketchup,
  lit a table's candle
and waited for the evening shift.

Flightless Bird

I know I don't hold road
as sacred as hawk must hold
air, but driving through Bald Eagle
State Forest I must have glimpsed
a little of that wind religion.

*

Warblers strum the instruments of their bodies
in rivergrass fresh with snake musk.
They are belting,

                all of them belting,

We are here!

      We are here!

            Yes this is where we are!

*

This is what I want to be—
an extension of something here,
something now—that sweet something
that won't grasp you or be grasped—
that dark, sugary, evolving something.
It's that air, that road
between my ribs.

*

I know the exact size of my bones
the way hawk knows angle,
circumference, the perfect art
of circle. It's the inherent knowledge,
the only religion we can believe in

by praying solely within the cathedrals
of our own bodies.

*

                        And who,
after seeing the flowing
and dipping, gliding
and gyring, can argue that hawk
is not an extension of air?

*

The spruce rise like nine thousand steeples
and if I could stop this car on this road
that never seems to end
I would kneel before this blue altar of sky.

Yes, this is where I am,
the religion I know for now.
It is found in the personal,
the slow revelations that have always
        been true for me,
the ones I'm just coming to
                now
        in this state forest.

And here, in the cracked angling
        of pines,

a wind stirs up inside me.

*

Drunk Again, I Stumble Home on Euclid and Cut Across Thornden Park Baseball Field

I.

Tonight the trees bend over like broken
old women picking up their husbands'
empty whiskey bottles.
The film of sky never
runs out of frames, never
runs out of dynamism & greased movement—
it moves quicker than my blood.
Doesn't it always come to this?—an awareness
dancing with my great ignorance. How right now
underfoot
the moles are squealing,
dying, making love, sliding through the dirt
that holds me up, holds these trees up,
holds itself back, compact,
and how goddamn strong the sky is—
how sky holds up planets
like polished marbles shot into dark grass.

A barn owl slides down from the sky
onto a mouse—just like that.
I round third
and head for home.

II.

Tomorrow I will wake to vacancies
I know every inch of,
a camera full of negatives;
dead whiskey will swirl inside me

like a warm rain stirs the sky
before sky flashes down onto pavement,
soaks the mailman, pours over
growling dogs, drenches car dealers,
and affects everything that walks through
with its perfect wetness.

Bleeding Jesus

Sitting in catechism, the priest punching Jesus
    into our heads, I stared into the dank hallway
beside the room. My attention snapped

to my hands, rapped by Father Longinus's ruler.
    He talked about the cross, the thorns,
the slow driving of nails. It was the pain

that interested my nine-year-old mind,
    the coincidental pain of our hands—
hard, deliberate. I ran home

and told my mother that I was Jesus, the Son of God.
    She slapped me twice and banished me
to my room, which only convinced me I was Christ.

The next day, I told some classmates
    I was Jesus. They didn't believe me
until I named them my apostles—

Saint Hank, Saint Milo, Saint Fat Eddie.
    I was ready now for the pain, the crucifixion.
We met at Happy's Ice Cream Parlor for a last supper—

the cone was my body, chocolate fudge my blood.
    We all had seconds. We couldn't find
a good cross, so they tied me

to a swingset in the schoolyard. I told them
　　to leave me. They acted sad,
as was planned, and left.

As the night gathered itself, I started
　　feeling lonely, hungry. My arms tired
from the spread I was in—the opening of an embrace

that was never able to close, to enwrap.
　　How prone a god can be.
I noticed a patch of wild blossoms

at my feet. They were small, purple.
　　They looked easy to kick up, so open
and convenient—their thin, sweet petal-meat

would be a wafer on my tongue. And I thought
　　of why I was there, how it was no fun
being Jesus. I left the blossoms where they were,

as I had found them, and screamed
　　for someone to get me, to untie me,
for it to be finished.

Something You Haven't Found

The world is okay, Karen,
so put down the gun.
When all the right things are too soft
and the worse things are hard—
when you touch your life
and it gives too easily,
like an eaten-out peach
that should be thrown from the barrel—
when you're a fire waiting to blaze
but can't find the kindling—
the world is okay.
Even when the tight muscle of sky
relaxes
and hail hails all over—
who could have guessed there's so much
hardness in the air?—
the world is still okay.

＊   ＊

It is the softness you want.
In fields, you revel
in the chicken hawk's wide circles—
you say they encompass your heart—
but you turn away from the fantastic descent
upon a bluebird, much preferring
the easier part of nature—
say, the slow, slow bulbing of tangerines
on a low branch, or the kiss of water
upon a river oak's root.

*   *

We come from the water
and what could be softer?
The stream behind my house
divides at the bed of sand
and rain will lay its weight
in the slightest of my lawn's small valleys.
Water will pull through the tiniest cracks
of anything you own
and tongue them clean.
And still it can drag canyons out of solid plains
    and put out fire.
Yes—the soft can wear away the hard,
so put down the gun.

*   *

Sometimes we get caught up
in the hardness—it nets us,
scratches our lives. My uncle
chose death in an inn after my aunt
had left him. The bartender said
he sat down, seemingly sure of everything
he wanted, and ordered a shot of Sambuca—
the sweetest shot in the house.
While the bartender poured it, my uncle
pulled out his army pistol
and blew that flame into his own dampness.
Death must be hard, Karen—
it can scatter anything—
and that's why I choose life.

It's full of softness—
it flows into valleys
and leans toward the moon.
How it steals up at an intimate moment
between lovers,
and can go away as quick and jarringly
as a newborn calf's neck
can snap.

　　　　　✳　　　　✳

And so when death becomes a soft word
in your too-perfect ear,
when you lift it up
and put its nozzle in your mouth,
when you think it can make you blaze,
let your tongue ride its hardness—
know right down to your fingertips
at the end of that trigger
lies nothing you can hope will be
better, softer, more reassuring
than life. All I can tell you, Karen,
is that the world is okay.
The world is okay.
When secrets slip out,
secrets you didn't even know about—
when surprise and vulnerability
kiss on your doorstep
and desperation frequents your windows,
pull them to you. Squeeze them
into your chest and know
the softness it takes not to be hard.

When you have eaten everything
you can think to eat—
when your cupboards are empty
and your garbage is full
and you're still hungry
for something you haven't found—
put down the gun.
When the world is a tidal wave
nearing your block and your house
doesn't seem as sound as it once did—
put down the gun.
A sycamore bent with hard wind
will still bend back
and will embrace that wind
with all its leafiness,
let itself be pulled,
feel the slash and tug
of its own weight,
and will still bend back
when hard wind turns soft.

*

Anima

She leads me into an empty bar
where the juke box records haven't changed
for years, where we could slow dance
on a stool and, when she's drunk enough,
she could tell me how she needs to love me.
What does she want?—she wants what every woman
in my life wants—for me to stop being such a jerk,
and I know this. I tease her with my maleness
just to keep her on her toes. Tonight
we've got a date—we're meeting for dinner,
where we'll negotiate once again our separate needs,
trade secrets, decide how to walk perfectly, no tripping,
almost a ballet of silent touchings and consequence.
I'm bringing the wine, she's bringing everything
she knows I'll be lacking.

Inspiration

It crosses me three

times and wraps me like

Jesus in words and the

places between words, the

inspired, breathed-in

places that are found

in all of us, the spirit

of lightning—it connects us

like words, connects the

words like something connects

us—creation, creation.

Love on the Assembly Line

The assembly line would keep going,
   even when he fell behind
production.
        As he filled the boxes he knew
          he was full of her.

But the warehouse was no place
                for love,
   and that made him a rebel
for bringing love in.

   The workers knew something was up—
he opened doors for them,
      he drank his coffee slow,
   he was always late on Thursdays.

When they approached him about it—
   when they had him
      and his love in a corner—
they wanted to know everything.
   And, because he was so full
of what they needed,
      he gladly gave it up.

The workers took it all,
   labeled it, put it on the line
to disassemble it, see how it ticked.
They lined up
   the length of the factory, and with this chain
      they held the love down,

took it apart one nut at a time,
                    examined every screw.
Soon a piece of his love was in everybody's hands
    and their hands started to hum
            with his broken down heart.

They never gave it back to him—
            instead they took their pieces of love,
    placed it in other things—
        cars, stereos, generators—
some ate lunch
            with the love they'd never share,
    some brought it home
            and put it on a proud mantle,
and some voted for the president with their love.

And as far as he is concerned,
    he whose love is in the hands of others,
he trolls the evening streets
            looking for what may be discarded—
a leg, perhaps,
        that his love used to stand on,
    or maybe a battery.
The hand that held his love
            now collects time and callouses,
    and at the factory
everyone is happy again,
            everyone filling boxes,
            everyone pushing buttons,
    everyone doing what is necessary
            to assemble the perfect working machine.

A Few Good Lies for the Personals

First the easy ones:
I wrote the great American poem.
I am a millionaire. I am so handsome
you will be afraid to touch me
but I am humble enough to let you,
      and then some.

But *too* easy—only something more subtle
can match my best badness.
If I were to lie, I would tell you
I would hurt you—that your heart
will never be broken
as roughly as in my hand,

and you might be intrigued.

I will tell you how I pray
   that your skin be my only redemption—
how I will spread over you
             farther than the rivers—
with more energy than the world's most undiscovered ocean—
to make you wet with my badness
 and watch the sun swing over your body,

and I'll swing it over again.

Yes, I'll lay the blocks of my immorality so high
    that your fences will be in no position to bargain.
Then I'll let my stones crumble,
         however you'd like;

let you see

      how low they can go—

how no threat, no psalm

      could ever bring a weight onto me

        as the truth of your fingertips can.

Saturday and She's Still Gone

The cup of black coffee sits on the morning newspaper
and it is mid-afternoon after a night of sleeplessness.
The clichés race around my mind like wild dogs
running through a house they won't leave
and I can't kick them out: "Pick up the pieces,"
"Life goes on," "Fish in the sea"—
yeahyeahright. Sayitagain, sayitagain.
That doesn't explain how an absence
can be such a presence, how all night
that absence lay down with me, rolled over,
spread itself across my face and wouldn't
let me sleep until morning drooled
its ugly light all over me and another day.
Those clichés burn the toast with me
and curse the cat with me right out
the catdoor into the world of rain and fuckheads,
but they don't say how loneliness has piled up
and is spilling over the sugarbowl
as I reach for a spoonful of sweetness.
Those clichés walk down Broad with me
but don't account for the gall in my chest
pockets, the bitterness I pull out and rub my head with
as I pass two lovers here, two there, on a bench,
a bus, a corner, a parking lot, a newsstand,
another corner, near a mailbox, a plugged gutter,
plugged against the rain and sun
and greasy pollution Syracuse spits up
to that great Nothing of sky all morning
and evening and day as I walk

with my eyes open but mouth closed—
no reason to open this mouth—
none at all—no lips to touch,
no kind words to put out—I'll just shut up now
(yeahyeahright, sayitagain, sayitagain),
open to page two—maybe fold the wash
in a little bit, maybe call her
"bitch" or "baby" or something
a little more truthful, maybe do nothing.

Delaware Water Gap, NJ Side, Election Year, Rush Hour, Hungry Again

The sun slips like a tongue
   down the sky's neck
and the flowers within me

open to it all.
   The world has lost its money
so I have wandered into these crags,

tall pitch pine, ascended
   the shins and thighs
of this state to escape the bars

where drunken laughter is overcome easily
   by the things of this sober world,
where the television's wide embrace

pulls us into lay-offs and mortgages.
   The entire arm
of the Delaware reaches for an ocean

as the cars of our lives reach for something
   we each call home.
Right now in Hampton, my floor is filled

with lottery tickets, sweepstakes
   forms, fast money that is always
six numbers away. I've left that for now

to be part of this larger body. There is something urging
    about the silhouettes of silos
standing in the setting sun. I will be part

of this mountain—I will budge
    only when the entire skin of this cliff
budges—avalanche or the subtle rubbings

of erosion. I will do well to make
    like this cliff—that egg—
a tree, a cloud—where what is larger

sings in accordance
    with our smaller concerns,
where the gap is what we cannot believe,

where sky can offer a constance
    of nothing,
and where the bushes

won't grow fatter each year,
    their dumb, prone, and delicate lungs
full of this less rich air.

Monopoly

There's something sad about the steam
pouring out the tenement vent.
Puerto Rican lovers double down
the steps into the concrete dusk.
Baked negroes look for shirts
and children stare at squirrels,
amazed at the mundane.
Broken windows are like black eyes,
wine bottles drop like dreams.
Fire hydrants stand forever—
statues of heroes that never were.
Between walls,
wet sheets are hung to dry—
at night they can't be seen
through the fog.

On the other side of the night,
some guy doubles down
and loses a hundred on
the turn of a card.
Close your eyes—
fat men belch like frogs
at the shore of a pond
filmed with flies.

This is Just to Slay
(a song of 1992)

I raised your taxes exorbitantly
and then cut them
after you were starving.

    Forgive me—
    the steak I bought with my senator's salary
        was so hot and juicy,
    and the wind that blows through the capitol
        is so cold.

In Defense of Syracuse's Loose-Knitted Sky

When the heat drops from the sun and needs no gravity to land
    hard and bounces off the hood of your old Volvo the way holy
    thoughts are rejected by the hard shell of science—

When prairie fire swings its hot arms into your fields and sings its
    falsetto into your sky and your house, your dog, your cigars
    and your lemonade just stand there in the path of heat's
    widening circle—

When heat crouches low, a heavy, pregnant beast full of
    destruction, and crawls up the road, softening the hardest
    blacktop, scorching the sideweeds, scratching stretch marks
    behind its wide berth,

slithers up your body and spills down your throat
    like a 90 proof shot of yesterday's thirst—

When heat does this, get your ass to Syracuse.
Go to Syracuse in February, say, when no one is thirsty, when heat
    is just an enigma like the promised word of God to the
    Zionists.

Stay there.
And when it snows, when the skies have carried the Great Lakes to
    you and dropped them like the Earth's soiled white laundry all
    over your front lawn and pet chihuahua—Syracuse's prank on
    all its people—

Think about Rt. 44 in South Dakota, how heat's ugly dogs will
    run into your car, pop your radiator, blow into your engine,
    and leak their dry cracks all over your leather interior.

And when sky falls down in April thirty drops at a time all over
    your freshly washed bicycle, think about the lopsided sky over
    Phoenix, all sun and glare and spilling sunburns,
    no rain,   no water,

            no water—

Heat can bake your pie,
but it can't build your filling.
It can rub your neck raw
but it can't kiss your body—
what kind of lover is that?
Let rain be your lover.
Let the many mouths of the sky
drop onto and suckle your body
in your body's many small places.
Let the rain heal you—let it lick you out of the bad mood
you bought in L.A. and can't exchange.
Let it fill you past your full mark.
Let it grow in your groin, spill into your spleen.
Let the rain form waterfalls where your body needs to laugh,
and let the waterfalls sprout up like orgasms on a good night.
Let yourself be so full of the sky's good humor
that even the snow, happy and awkward
in its own many bodies, is no surprise—
how the rain, put against the dryest,
most miserable of land and thoughts,

can cause tulips, turnips, potatoes and rainbows—
great colors bordering our rooves, crossing our town.
Let the rain water your spirit and let your spirit
continue to rain on others.
Indeed, let our spirits open as wide as our umbrellas—
how umbrellas are both male and female,
like any blooming flower.
Joy to the world. It is raining.
And the moments of our lives run deepest,
like our favorite valleys,
where they are most moist.

Dissatisfaction with Great Expanse

(a cry for long-distance lovers)

To know that our bodies are on the same highway
        but two time zones apart
does me no good.

    Distance has placed a roadblock
        on the freeway—
    a lump in our mashed potatoes.

The highways of America don't interest me—
        I'm much more interested
in the freeways of your body—
    the turnpike that runs down the front of your neck,
over your clavicle,
        between your pure, untouched breasts
    where I'd gladly make a pit stop,
along the ridge of your stomach,
        and will take me—

        I've been there before—

        into your great continental divide.

That is when I will be connected
    by highways with you—
how our roads will converge,

                not fork,
    where the hard asphalt softens with the day's heat
    and the toll taker puts his hand out
        expecting the kind of money

    you gladly waste in exotic nations.

Some Kind of Storm

Last night a hurricane blew into Lafayette, Lafayette
   where Sara and I once lay
with the wet angels in the tall grass
      on the banks of Rt. 10.

All of Louisiana shivered at midnight
   when the storm hugged its banks,
      questioned its borders,
blew all sensibility and orientation
      to a place known only by the damned and certain dogs,

and the City of New Orleans shook
   with a new kind of music.
The houses started to dance, a rumba
      with dips
         followed by a stillness
     New Orleans didn't know.
And it was just another dance to that city of fedoras and pregnant women.

But in Lafayette, Lafayette
   dropped its accent for a wind
as cajun spices blew up into small whirls—
     curry in the sky
   came raining over the highways
and drivers cried all the way home.

And all I could think of was
Sara's mouth, how lost I became in her pocket of moans,
   how that night a storm stirred up in my chest, my legs,
my arms, as I lifted her and her own storm

into the soft grass, below the headlights
        and noise of the passionless.
How our storms diverged, drenched everything,
and how all this was finally equalled in Lafayette

by Andrew, Prince of Motion,
        as he shoved into walls,
                broke through rooves,
driving everything,
                relentless,
        to get to the heart of the city,
to throw some spices in the air like a dangerous confetti
        only lovers and certain dogs could appreciate;

and how Andrew, when Andrew left, took
        Lafayette with him, and dissipated only with distance
and the promised fading memory
        as generations grow older, forget,
fall out of love,
                build houses they'd improve on,
        and settle for them.

A Note To Karen

It's in our hands, our
voices, the spontaneous moments
we wait for, build with.
It may be as small as a sweep
of hair on an unexpecting arm, or
as large as my glance into yours.
It is in the small moves and pauses,
and the movements in the pauses.
It is the whittling, the allowed
carving, the shaping
to allow slips, the molded hollows
in us worn from containing
and releasing, holding and letting be.

The Dying of the Light

The pine barrens 50 miles south of us
kill themselves every ninety years.
The way they live—hoarding sunlight
and rain—pirating away the lesser
parts of the woods until only the fewer giants
remain, making a thinner forest.
And Father, you've done it now.
You've smoked and drank and smoked
and drank your way right into the body
you're dying in—the body that frames you
but no longer supports you. It's broken—
it's breaking you. It's full of shadows
and caves where it should be solid and overgrown
with a body's own full-rooted days.
Empty, empty—a bloated, empty shell, full
of echoes that ring "empty, empty," full
of echoes whispering woods' crooked intent.
Like the pine barrens. Yes, the pine barrens.
When winter drags its calloused ass down
the bark, its fingers of ice scratching their way
behind, brittle needles fall to earth and wait
for that one leg of electric sky to tromp their thirsty bodies.
And then the flames. And then there's more
flames. And you still smoke now,
lying in this hospital room. In light
of all this, what can be said? The walls
are cleaner than your insides. You know
it's getting late. Pill to sleep. Needle to live.
Father, in every woods there runs an evil,
a Jimmy Leeds★ who'll stir up the ground

with whispers that become echoes in later years.
And then this: one is left lying in one's rotting,
incinerable forest. And below one's back,
every needle has a horrible secret.

* Jimmy Leeds—the name of "The Jersey Devil," a creature in Pine Barren folklore.

To Grandmother,
After a Photograph of Joseph Cornell

Man is no longer water to me; he is
light: the soft light of a bird's belly

or the slow filter of lace curtains. He
is found in windows and mirrors, weakens

in corners and the tint of memory.
                                        Whatever light
you were, you had,   whatever—

it's gone. There was water at the wake,
tears over your shell, but—I will not lie—

there was light. Hard, undulating light—
the insincerity of relations, the cold light

reflected from dead flesh.
                            And I know
the danger of being light in light, drowning

in it like water. I go to the dark sea,
stand on a crag, wait. The balance is here—

the undetectable places where rock ends
and sea begins, where sea and sky lick,

where the moon drools thick
on passing clouds, and the stars spear everything

and nothing. I stared into your eyes,
two flashing seagulls. Here, gone.

It is the dimness I fear.

Yellowstone

The lake is a riddle—
it asks itself over and over again.
To know the answer, you must own water—
even the water of your own body
would suffice. The lake beckons to be heard
as only the lonely can hear it—
a radio signal with a very specific destination.
It throws itself onto the shore
at your feet—are you lonely enough
to answer it yet? The answer lies
in how well you throw yourself
into the water. There are answers
in the depths—loves to be reckoned with.
Look again at the flat promise
of so much water—how it will swallow
you, all of you, like rain.
This lake is a riddle—
it asks itself over and over again.

Movement

It is noon and the farmer is dying.

The sun presses the barn's broad chest

and hot chickens breathe. The wheatfields

breathe. A haziness falls every-

where—it fills the wheelbarrow, mats

down horsetails, rubs against the stones.

Mud cracks and sleeps, cracks again. The barn door

wheezes open. In the hayloft, wet kittens squint.

Life in the Blue Danube

san francisco, July 1992

The sidewalk stretches into its own
cat-like tendencies, and the waitress
knocks over a chair.

        There is my world,
the beginning of it—
        if Kevin were here,
there might be a yellow-tinted drunk
slumped against a parked Subaru,
or something he'd wish to invent
but not let himself.

        There—Kevin is now
a part of our world, reader,
and now so are you.
        If I could,
I would let this poem call out
to every corner of our puny sky
and pull in ornate onks, boomerangs,
slow-moving glaciers.
        If I could
this poem would stretch out, too,
and on it we could walk
right into the next page,
    where possibilities stick to your smile, run through your teeth
    just as bag ladies pirouette through Indiana cornfields.
Invent. If you already know it,
there's no reason to write it.

The Artist in New Orleans:
Storm Showers Rain Wet

The egret on the state line
   craned its neck to the soggy sky
and saw, maybe, what was to be
   a spectacular sunset
         if not for the hurricane—
   the sky was something like a seed
      from which light could eventually grow,
   could fall
      over the fields, over the beans,
over the cows slowly rising
   to move to their feed,
also wet now, as is the scarecrow,
   the land itself, the many bridges
people make everyday,
   to travel over what the rain
      has made before—

Bourbon Street was growing louder with its own nature,
   and soon the sky
         and all it held
would tickle the city's pavement,
                would dance
over the egret, around its strained neck,
   and over the many seeds
      the egret is looking over—
   each seed a whisper
      of more rain to come,
      of wet possibilities, of sproutings,
         of more poems to be,

more words to be born
with pursed lips
and swinging hips,
words that carried umbrellas
but forsook them
just to dance with the freedom
empty bottles are filled with
when a storm shakes them into a music
they never contained
or rattled
before.

The Fury

In high school, boys who aren't bad do bad things
    just to not be good.
This is the way it was that day we rebelled
    against the cafeteria,
much preferring the Burger King, two towns away.
    I had just bought my first car,
a 1970 Plymouth Fury, and, although it was tested,
    I wanted to test it. Mr. Burns, who it was rumored
didn't have any hair on his balls, walked the parking lot
    like Cerberus during lunch, waiting, watching
for bad people, trying to keep them in school
    near the good kids. We didn't care,
and once we made it to the Fury my key broke
    into her ignition as if it were the first time,
and when I turned it she hummed alive, her V-8 heart
    catching Cerberus's ear.
But it was too late for him—our badness had started
    and now it rolled onto the street, the motor gassed, revved.
It was beautiful—the reckless, dizzy, happy motion exercised
    by my rods, exemplified by Sharon on my lap,
Sharon who would sit on the lap of anybody that was skipping school
    or had a car, and God I was doing both!
Tim and Carla were in the back, his tongue already down
    her throat, the wind filling the car,
Sharon's hair filling my face, her hand on my crotch,
    the curve in my pants, the curve in the road,

47

it was all so right, so perfect—
     the swing of the car, the slow swift arc
of the world, Tim biting Carla's tongue, the spin
     waking him from his dizzy lust,
my Fury backwards, the pipe music created
     when rubber and pavement feel each other out
to a stop.
     When we got back to school,
there was hairless Cerberus, ushering us back to hell,
     our Fury tested, the curves in us
that needed to be swung swung, the four of us bad
     for good.

Romance, Exactly as I Remember It,

is how
the moon rises
full
every night
and the line it marches
is always taut
with hopes of young lovers
tonguing their troubles
into a place their mouths
can hardly contain.
The rising moon knows
every kiss
ever made between fire escape bars,
it knows every Johnny Mathis tune,
it knows absolutely
nothing else.
It empties itself
every 28 days,
and that is why
young lovers
feel new
as the tide pulls up
onto their feet
like a blanket
they will never toss off.

In their mouths,
in the moon's mouth,
promises are discovered
amid salt and sugar,

and all these white things
swell into a larger kiss
that will eclipse
only in the shadow
of their own smart,
slowly-travelling
bodies.

(after Edwin Romond)

Guilt

It sneaks up on you,
maybe lies in your bed.
It whispers three good reasons you are a bastard:
    for all you've stolen,
    for all you've done to her,
    and for pissing on Mrs. Johnson's cat last night.
You ask if there's some mistake—
    it moans at the stupidity of your asking.
You ask to remedy your bastardhood.
It is then that it stands upright,
        200 feet tall,
looks down,
        sticks its giant toenail
    through the one part of your body
        you've always held as sacred,
and bolts the shrinking door shut.

It is now just you and your guilt,
    stuck in this room,
no card games,
            nobody talking,
staring at each other,
    waiting for the answers
that neither has the power to give.

Coming Clean

The phone rings. A woman tells me I'm doomed,
she has a voodoo doll of me,

and hangs up. Immediately I know it's true—
I've been having pains for weeks.

My wife would have nothing to do
with these aches, and referred me to my mother,

who insisted on having everything to do with them.
So I went to the doctor, who put my pain

under lights, opened it, listened to it,
descended into it with all his technology

and found nothing. This is how it deepened.
Whatever it was, I knew it wasn't something

to be found in the local, the body.
When the call came long distance with my answer,

I was actually grateful. Now I turn
to the windowsill, to the pile of chain letters

from Latvia I've been receiving, the ones
I haven't been mailing forth, and know

this is all connected, how the tide of black magic
can cross any ocean. I am a sinner

and turn back the clock of my heart
to recount all my heart-felt sins—

the ones that, if there is a hell,
and if it isn't like this, might itch a little

for punishment. The time I felt my friend Karen's ass,
wanting her more than any car, even at 17.

I apologized later, but we know how those things go.
The only thing I regretted was that she didn't like it.

So I apologize now. And to Mr. Romond,
11th grade English teacher who promised us all

Look Homeward, Angel would get better.
I'm sorry, Mr. Romond, for I have sinned.

All eight hundred pages of your book,
which I said I lost, are ashes

somewhere in an old campfire pit.
That night, literaturg made me feel so warm.

And the great poet, Stephen Dunn—I won't tell you
what I've done—just know it was horrible,

and you never realized it anyway.
These are all petty larcenies of the heart—

small pleasures I've stolen and can't give back,
or wouldn't. The letters accumulate, and the pains

I take to right my life grow sharper.
In the distance, BJ Ward is a doll

and that image is tearing me apart.

The Classics in Couplets

(Written after overhearing a student complain, "Cliff notes are too long.")

The Odyssey

He got lost.
He paid the cost.

Hamlet

Uncle married mother.
　Oh brother!

Waiting for Godot

I don't hear him comin'—
Boy, am I bummin'.

The Love Song of J. Alfred Prufrock

No calls for a week.
Am I a geek?

Oedipus Rex

Oh brother—
I married mother!

Afraid of My Own Snoring

(for George Cruys)

20 too far behind and 30
around the corner, I went into the woods
alone. The fire was small but sufficient
enough to warm but not hurt me.

The burnt-edged hot dog was good, better
because of hunger, and the clouds held promise
enough for me to pitch my tent. If wind
blew strong, I would have to lie and let her

do what damage was in her invisible, fluid,
long bones. The tent flapped its skins
for hours, and the whole world
about me became alive—too alive. Wood

became less hard, softened with my own startled blood.
And, as I started to sleep, an enormous bear
came to my tent, moaned a low hungry tone,
enough to stir me from the gourmet, home-cooked food

I was lying with in my dreams.
I checked outside, swung my flashlight
all around, saw nothing but woods
that now seemed still. Even the breeze

had stopped. Settling back to sleep,
the bear came again, this time closer
than he sounded before, with his low threatening
groan. I jumped from my sleep, not as deep

as the darkness around me, and again
spread my light, my only weapon against the dark

and the things the dark held. Again, nothing
came of it. It happened twice more, the sleep and the din

of the bear's throat, and still there was nothing in it.
I did not sleep anymore after that—just lied
waiting for the bear's return. He never came,
I never slept, and wasted the meat of the night.

As I left the woods at dawn, it occurred
to me how that bear came only when it knew,
somehow, my eyes were elsewhere, somewhere
inward, and that is when he could be heard.

The bear, the woods, everything threatening was still—
I should have slept more soundly through my fears
in the trees—looked inward, and stayed there, instead
of being shook and ruled by such an invisible thrill.

A Quiet Day in Newark

Finally—finally I can hear the birds.
They chirp slowly. They sound like chimes made of sugar.
All the cars have stopped.
People are standing in doorways,
motionless. I hear the birds—they are beautiful.
A block away there is a woman crying. All this
is all I hear. She cries as if her mouth were the only door
to let pain out her body. The grammar school across the street
never makes noise—it has no windows to let in light
or bullets. A young man sticks his head out
a tenement window, slowly—a bead of sweat runs from his shiny head
onto the uneven sidewalk below. One woman's shoe lies unperturbed
on Clinton. Another person, this one also a woman,
moves silently from a candy shop. Her eyes move quickly,
side to side—two startled animals. A car starts crawling up Clinton
again, and I still peer from behind my dashboard.
There is headshaking now, nervous laughter
from men who almost live in hardware stores. Yes, now the world
seems to be rotating again—there is movement
in cars, on foot, in baby carriages.
I sit up straight, just as I was
before the four teens came running down the alley,
swinging guns like banners for freedom
in a war I've not fought. I shift
into drive, let my foot off the brake,
move slowly up Clinton, just as I was
before these four children brought life
into this dead city, blasting noise out, ricocheting
into pavement and flesh, moving all bystanders inside

themselves, tucked under cars, arches, the wings
we have grown and carry not to fly with
but to keep ourselves hidden.

Instant Sundance

(Lakota Sioux Rosebud Reservation,
July 24-27, 1992)

for Tim Provencal

Take a tree—a great tree—
    hang parts of your life from it.
Friends will help.

Move your feet a little—
    a little in all directions.
As you travel outward, travel inward.

Before, during, and after,
    you must sweat.
Pour out all your poisons and promises

and love the human nation.
    Once you are dry
of hubris, of fear of disappointment,

once you have washed yourself
    with the rocks and water
you dredge up from inside,

you must become equally hard and soft
    until "balance" is the dance
you do with the tree in the changing wind.

You must know when to lift—
    let your body fill the sky as birds do—

know when to place, each footstep

a bucket of soul emptying into the earth
    as the sky fills the tree.
Thank the circle you're in—

thank the ground for its wide embrace,
    thank the sisters and brothers around you,
holding flowers like important messages,

and thank your own body, a temple today—
    the hands for clearing the land,
the torso for moving in holy sentences,

the hair for flying like your spirit,
    your breath for massaging the chapel,
and your throat, your waterless throat,

for carrying the wind to your lungs,
    for carrying your scream to Grandfather,
and for the scream itself, punctuating

like part of a lost heartbeat
    that all doctors had given up on,
now suddenly glowing in the medicine of the breeze.

Letter To Some Students Whom I May Never See Again After a Five Day Writing Workshop

When you suffer, I hope you suffer miserably.
Is that what is appropriate here?
When you love, I hope you love without hope.
When happy, I hope you are blind

    only some of the time.

                I hope your emotions
become the ocean

        you have only half-charted;
let them bathe you with their unknown waters,
and let those waters run as deep and long

    as you can possibly bear.

           You want advice?
Let your pen be a life-line,

    let it bleed

        where you have been most cut,
or where you most need to cut yourself.

Is my metaphor too grand? Perhaps your pen
    should never be more than pen. Perhaps you
should always realize that. Perhaps your pen
    should be what you never leave—

        let your words live without you.

    Be the mother who has lost the child
to the world it must now be a part of.
Be the father who never knew the child anyway.

Stand on the shores of your poems and wave goodbye
as the waters carry that craft to the end of its world,
    where surely it will plunge into nothing.

And if there is dirt,
                if the craft strikes land,
        may the discovery of that New World
            be a constant surprise
                    that carries you inland,

and as you discover the pools inside you
            may you explore them with the same thirst.

To be human is to let go the hand of God,
        and so you, the creator, have to let your work be human:
            let the reader have your words,
                let emotion examine its own name.
        Let the hope of nothing,   of an end,
                be where you begin.
        When letting go,
                    say goodbye with both hands.

Dancing with the Teacher

(for Maureen Kosa)

What a fiery teacher she was!
    Not knowing any better,
I engaged her

in verbal banter—she loved Huck Finn
    and I loved Huck Finn
and the whole class,

the whole world could go to hell
    for all I cared.
She took the first step and I took

her hand and soon we were rocking on that raft
    with Huck and Jim, doing the rumba,
the jitterbug, the twist—

we got down and let out—
    we didn't stop
with the whole class gawking,

amazed that literature could shake us,
    that mere words
could create such dizzy abandon,

could move us so violently,
    our bodies twenty years apart
but so close together, in sync.

When Shakespeare entered the room

we turned the lights low,
pulled down the shades,

did a slow waltz, timing our dips
      with Hamlet's,
our shifts with Petruchio's.

But when Whitman came along,
      forget it!
Open the windows! Throw on the lights!

We hucklebucked, hully gullied, shook, shimmied,
      and locomotioned! We swung our bodies
and never let down!

The class was amazed—
      some caught on quick,
took that heat in,

and soon everyone broke loose—
      the charleston! the boogaloo! the handjive!
Mrs. Kosa madisoned, Jen Faber mashed potatoed,

Jake and Brett tangoed—even Jerome Higgins stood up
      and did the watusi!
Everyone was dancing

with the freedom hips were born with,
      the freedom of knees,
arms, torsos, necks—

the freedom to read

in other people's moves
a wildness greater than our own,

and the freedom to pick up,
    to learn how to be that wild
with our own steps in time.

Learning German

In German class they tell me about stressed places,
how my diction is too soft—that the language
can only be spoken with hard and soft.
There's half a globe making hard sounds,
saying the same things the other half does
with softer sounds—our thoughts are the same.

*   *

A girl with a hard tongue kissed me once.
It was new, different—she seemed old in my mouth.
It was outside, in her backyard—
there was no moon, no stars—I wallowed
between her rigidness and the cool hug
of the earth. When it was over,
there was some of my softness
in her, some of her hardness in me.

*   *

If I whisper
    marrow, pelt, horn
would you understand
somehow?

*   *

I know parents who start loving softly
and realize how hard it is.
                              It
starts the same—a look, a word,
a fist—they are soon full of fists.
They say Love is hard. I say love
was never meant to be all-soft or all-hard—

There is paper in oaks,
and oaks in paper.
It is the moment we look at it
that matters—what form we catch it in.

              *   *

We differ only in softnesses,
   and where they are,
and how these places
   are affected by hardness.

              *   *

I know men who are moments,
who tried to love hard and found
how soft it is.
                    You know
them too—maybe in some bar,
maybe your lunchroom, maybe
you've been loved by one
or raised someone who was.
They're the men who sit in corners
and smell whiskey-thick—they're

the assured moments of a place you frequent,
the moments you try to avoid.
They crouch and mutter to themselves,
turning and watching their hands
whose palms wear the slow blankets of callouses.

✳   ✳

We differ only in hardnesses,
   and where they are,
and how these places
   are affected by softness.

✳   ✳

Have you ever lived your life hard/soft?
Perhaps in your work, or your love?
The way your hand touches, responds, touches—
the way your tongue moves when you speak.
Have you ever learned to say "fuck"
to your lover? Surely you know the balance
of hard and soft, where they touch,
and how they bend to meet.

✳   ✳

And my tongue wants to bend like that,
wants to have both marrow and horn, palms
and knuckles, wood and pulp—
it wants to border them,
ride out the space between them,
and moisten everything it touches.

This is how I will learn German;
how, like any language,
it must be spoken with everything I have.

*

The Appendix Poem

Have you taken out what won't work?
Have you prodded it,
          made sure it was deathly sick?
     Did you wash your hands first?

Have you severed and dissected, seen its dirt?

               You still don't know, do you?

          Its secret is an explosion,
                    not a nick.

And I've seen explosions better than you.

I've seen poems,
          so tell me,

                    did it burst?

Acknowledgments

These journals have published or will publish the following poems:

The Coastal Forest Review: "A Note to Karen," "Some Kind of Storm"

Defined Providence: "Movement"

Double-Entendre: "Anima," "Life in the Blue Danube"

The Hiram Poetry Review: "Bleeding Jesus," "Dancing with the Teacher"

Poet Lore: "To Grandmother, After a Photograph of Joseph Cornell"

The Sound Effects Newsletter: "In Defense of Syracuse's Loose-Knitted Sky," "Inspiration," "Monopoly"

South Trenton Review: "Coming Clean," " The Dying of the Light," "The First Thing to Say," "The Fury"

The Sun: "Drunk Again, I Stumble Home on Euclid and Cut Across Thornden Park Baseball Field," "Hometown: Alliance, New Jersey"

Also, "Monopoly" won the 1986 "Discovery" Poetry Contest of the YM-YWHA of North Jersey and was originally published in the winners' anthology.

"Letter To Some Students Whom I May Never See Again After a Five Day Writing Workshop" received a commendation in the 1992 Chester H. Jones Foundation National Poetry Competition and was originally published in the winners' anthology.

BJ Ward

Biographical Note

BJ Ward lives in Washington, New Jersey. He works in the Writers-In-The-Schools program, sponsored by the New Jersey State Council on the Arts, the Playwrights Theatre of New Jersey, and the National Endowment for the Arts. He earned his M.A. in Creative Writing at Syracuse University where he served as a University Distinguished Fellow and a Summer Fellow. He was one of ten writers nationally to be awarded a full scholarship for the Bucknell Seminar for Younger Poets in 1988.